From Writer to Author Series

Somebody!! Pleaseee! Help Me To Write

Erica & Lewis Rutherford Jr

Kingdom Writers Books

Indianapolis, IN

From Writer To Author Series

Somebody Please Help Me To Write!

Kingdom Writers Books
Indianapolis, IN 46221
317-426-7392
kingdomwritersbooks.wordpress.com
kingdomwriters2017@gmail.com

Copyright © 2018

All Rights Reserved. No part of this book may be reproduced, stored in a retrieval system, or transmitted by any means without the written permission of the authors.

Cover Images: Filmmaker-2838945_1280 & Work-management-907669_1280
Cover Image Design: Filmmaker-2838945_1280 | lukasbieri | Pixabay & Work-Management-907669_1280 | Shivmirthyu | Pixabay

ISBN-13: 9781731076632

Printed in the United States of America

Dedication

We dedicate this book to the ones who are inspired to write and want to become writers.

To the ones who always had a story to tell, a poem to express or something that encourages, empowers and help others to see the best in themselves and have desired to get it in their hands.

To those that have desired to go from being Writers to Authors and want their dream to become a reality.

To those who have been frustrated with the writing process and don't know where to pick up writing again.

To those who desire to start writing but don't know where to begin.

This book is mostly dedicated to our fellow Non-fiction authors or soon to be authors.

May this book not only help ignite your passion for writing, encourage on your writing journey and or help you get unstuck and writing again, but also inspire you to be An Author.

Acknowledgements

First, we acknowledge and give all honor and glory to our Lord and Savior Jesus Christ for giving us all the words to write for this book

To our publishing coach, teacher, mentor and friend; Julia A Royston, we want to thank you so much for everything. Because of you, your calling and your gift, is the reason this book is even possible. We thank God for you every day, and you and Brian are family. We have an audience to reach, so here we go.

To our mentor, Apostle Tracey George, You came at a time that was so needed in our lives. You truly helped, encouraged and inspired us not to give up. Thank you for helping to pull out of us what God placed there and the very things we almost gave up on. We love you and appreciate you. We say Thank you.

To our mother, mother-in-law and friend; Lois Rutherford, Thank you for believing in us and for sharing the vision that God gave you concerning us writing more books. You were truly our cheerleader and support through all the rough times we had just trying to get this book finished and published. Thank you for being there. We love you and Thank God for you every day.

To our family and friends that have encouraged and supported us in our writing journey as we have sought to do God's will in everything that we have done. We will continue to do great things.

Table of Contents

Dedication	**iii**
Acknowledgments	**iv**
Introduction	**viii**
3-2-1 Let's Start Writing	**1**
Today! Right Now! Let's Prepare	1
The Starting Point	1
Let's Begin!	1
What Moves You	1
Who's Your Audience	2
Now How Do I Begin	3
Puzzle Piece Writing	5
On Your March! Get Set! Go!	7
And We're Off! ~ Congratulations	9
Evaluation	10
Scheduling That Writing Date	**11**
Where Will You Write	11
Describe Your Writing Atmosphere	11
What Day and Time?	12
What Are Your Goals?	13
What's Your Approach?	14
Schedule Check It!	14

Congratulations 15

Relationship Building ~ Your Writing — 17

Identifying Your What 17

Determine Your Approach 18

Re-Examining Your Deadline 18

3 Writing Relationship Points 18

    You Must Show Up 18

    Keep Choosing Each Other 19

    Keep Your Eyes Focused ~Distractions Must Go! 19

    Your Writing Communication Examination 20

    A Tip To Keep Your Writing Relationship Fresh 21

Encouraging The Writer In You — 23

It's The Bravest Thing I've Ever Done 23

I Can Make A Difference (Yes You Can!) 23

I Can Make It Happen 24

I'm Just One Person, But An Important Person 25

EveryDay Is A Great Day To Write 26

I Must Show Up 27

Additional Affirmations 28

Help My Writing, Pleaseee! — 31

Understand, It Is Work 31

How Do I Communicate 32

Your Attitude, Your Approach, Your Writing	34
Pay Attention	36
Be You	37
Express Yourself	38
Help Me I'm Stuck	40
Oh No! I Missed My Writing Date	42
Did My Help Forsake Me?	43
When The Bitter End Is The Sweetest	45
Change Your View	46
It's A Wrap! ~ You Finished!	**47**
About The Authors	**49**
Bonuses	**51**

Introduction

How many times have you said to yourself, "I have a book I need to write" or simply, "I need to write a book?" You hear others talk about the book(s) they have written and it just reminds you of your book that you have yet to write. Maybe you have set down at various times throughout your life and written note after note, journal entry after journal entry or typed document after typed document and have yet to price it all together? Maybe you are one that has heard countless times the words, "You need to write a book?" Probably too many times, but what has set you back or held you up? Has it been fear or procrastination? Have you found yourself with no support through your writing journey? Have you even tried to seek out help? Well, it's time for all of that to change.

The major factor in you writing your book is, 'You.' Yes You! Writing a book requires a purpose, zeal, passion and a decision. There is a reason why you have come across this book. There is a reason why we have crossed paths. This workbook contains the help that you need and contains the information you need to start and complete the journey of writing your book.

Like you, before my husband Lewis and I became authors, we had no clue as to how to write a book. We had no identifiable help within our circle before meeting our coach and business mentor Julia Royston. Like you, we both had written lots of information in journals, on notepads, notebooks and within computer documents. We both knew we were called to write, but just didn't know where to begin nor what we should write on. So, the journey to writing our 1st book was real, raw and relevant. 1st, we figured out our purpose, identified the zeal and passion we both had and then made a decision. It was a big decision that required us to get a coach. That's right! A Coach, someone to help walk us through the process of writing and then later help publish our book. And it's this process, that we in return have been called to assist you with and through.

Hopefully this puts a smile on your face and causes a peace to come over you. Yes! Through the book, this workbook and even through additional available coaching, we are here to coach you through your writing journey with the end result being a completed manuscript. Yes, that's right. You are not here by accident. So sit, buckle up your seat belt and prepare yourself for the ride. Lewis and I are excited to be your coach through this journey. Your assignment is to read and complete all the exercises contained within the following pages. You can reach out to us for additional help along with journey as desired. Now, if you are all set, let's start our journey together. Here we go!

3-2-1 Let's Start Writing!

Today! Right Now! Let's Prepare!

Assignment: Read pages 1 through 4 in 'Somebody Please Help Me To Write Book' 1st before answering the questions.

Please answer the following questions.

Starting Point

What are my materials? Check All That Apply.

____Paper   ____Recording Device

____Pen   ____Typewriter

____Computer/Laptop   ____Quiet Spot/Your spot to write

Let's Begin!

If I had something to write about, what would it be?

What am I writing? ~Check one.

_____Poetry   ____Encouraging/Empowering Message

_____Story   ____Unsure

What Moves You?

What is the motivation behind your writing?

____Mom   ____Certain Experience

____Dad   ____Someone Else

____A Particular Problem   ____Other   What?_____

Who's Your Audience?

Question: Who do I want to reach or encourage with my message or story? Write your response here. Be as detailed and specific as possible.

Now How Do I Begin?

Exercise: Let's write for 20 minutes!

If you need more space, use a separate sheet of paper.

Puzzle Piece Writing

Assignment: Read pages 5 through 11 in Somebody Please Help Me To Write Book 1st before completing the exercise below.

Exercise

Here You Will Organize Your Writing

Write For Another 20 Minutes

Pair Up Those Words, Phrases and Relatable things and list them in the below columns.

Give each column a title that relates to the things within them.

Title_____   Title_____

- _____   - _____
- _____   - _____
- _____   - _____
- _____   - _____
- _____   - _____
- _____   - _____
- _____   - _____
- _____   - _____
- _____   - _____
- _____   - _____

If relates, put it in the same column.

Go through Everything you wrote down until everything is in a column.

Title_____   Title_____

- _____
- _____
- _____
- _____
- _____
- _____
- _____
- _____
- _____
- _____

- _____
- _____
- _____
- _____
- _____
- _____
- _____
- _____
- _____
- _____

Title_____   Title_____

- _____
- _____
- _____
- _____
- _____
- _____
- _____
- _____
- _____
- _____

- _____
- _____
- _____
- _____
- _____
- _____
- _____
- _____
- _____
- _____

If you need more space, use a separate sheet of paper.

On Your March! Get Set! Go!

Exercise: Write For Another 20 Minutes.

Begin writing on the organized sections

If you need more space, use a separate sheet of paper.

And You're Off!

Congratulations

You now have a working outline. Remember your Outline: is a guide to help you to work towards writing and completing your book. This may have been hard work, but you are well worth the Congratulations. Take a moment to Celebrate, and then prepare yourself to jump back in the flow and begin writing again.

Again Congratulations

Evaluation

Are you a 1st time writer?   Yes?_____   or   No?_____

Was this your 1st time writing in a while?   Yes?____   or   No?____

How do you feel after completing the 3 sets of 20-minute writings you just did?

Write your thoughts here.

_____

_____

_____

_____

Do you feel like you have built up a momentum to write your book?

Yes_____ or No_____

How excited are you?

A little_____   Somewhat_____   Very_____

Hopefully you are. You have done quite a bit of work already.

Now It's Time to Schedule Your Writing Times

Scheduling That Writing Date

Assignment: Read pages 13 through 16 in Somebody Please Help Me To Write Book 1st before completing the exercise below.

Exercise: Please answer the following questions:

Where Will You Write?

Check All That Apply.

__**Home:** Where?   ____Kitchen   ____Basement   ____Bedroom?

____Living Room   ____By the Fireplace

____Office   ____Park   ____Starbucks   ____Retreat Center

____Library   ____Library   ____Quiet Spot/Your spot to write

Describe Your Writing Atmosphere!

Write It Here.

_____

_____

_____

_____

_____

Include them when scheduling your writing dates

If you need more space, use a separate sheet of paper.

What Day and Time?

Exercise: **Pull out your calendar and write the days and times.**

Month:_____   Week of:_____

_____Monday   Time: _____and_____

_____Tuesday   Time: _____and_____

_____Wednesday   Time: _____and_____

_____Thursday   Time: _____and_____

_____Friday   Time: _____and_____

_____Saturday   Time: _____and_____

_____Sunday   Time: _____and_____

Where?_____

Atmosphere_____

Start with planning a week at a time, then if you need to re-adjust, then do so.

Month:_____   Week of:_____

_____Monday   Time: _____and_____

_____Tuesday   Time: _____nd_____

_____Wednesday   Time: _____and_____

_____Thursday   Time: _____and_____

_____Friday   Time: _____and_____

_____Saturday   Time: _____and_____

_____Sunday   Time: _____and_____

Where?_____

Atmosphere_____

What Are Your Goals?

Write it here.

Deadline?_____

Each week?_____

End of the Month?_____

End of 2nd Month?_____

What the rest of your goals here?

_____

_____

_____

_____

_____

_____

_____

If you need more space, use a separate sheet of paper.

What's Your Approach?

Assignment: Read pages 17 through 20 in Somebody Please Help Me To Write Book 1st before completing the exercise below.

Exercise: Check all that apply.

____Hand writing

____Paper ____Pen ____Pencil ____Notebook

____Voice Recording

____Hand-Held Recorder ____Computer Program ____Mobile Voice App

Typing

____Computer ____Typewriter ____Tablet ____Mobile Note App

Ghostwriting

____Friend ____Professional Ghost Writer

Schedule Check It!

Day of the Week for Tomorrow:_____

Time: _____and_____

Deadline: _____

Where? _____

Atmosphere_____

Your Approach _____

Congratulations

You should have now scheduled at least 2 weeks of writing. It is important that you continue to schedule out your writing sessions. Even if your schedule changes, continue to re-adjust and show up for your writing sessions. Remember to try and keep to your writing schedule which will help you to be more successful in completing your book. This may have been hard work, but you are well worth the Congratulations. Take a moment to Celebrate, and then prepare yourself to jump back in the flow and begin writing again.

Again Congratulations

Relationship Building ~ Your Writing

Assignment: Read page 21 in 'Somebody Please Help Me To Write Book' 1st before answering the questions.

The Writer + Writing = Love Relationship

Identifying Your 'What.'

Do have you the passion, fire or zeal to write your book? _____

Who or what is the motivation behind you writing your book?

_____

_____

_____

_____

You must have motivation to write your story!

Exercise: Take post cards and write out what motivates you on it.

Next, post it everywhere you can see it everyday.

Assignment: Read pages 22 through 24 in 'Somebody Please Help Me To Write Book' 1st before answering the questions.

Determine Your Approach ~ Circle Your Choice.

Are you going down the outline? ~ Little by Little

OR

Are you just writing on random parts of the outline? ~ Head On

What's Your Attitude Approach? ~ Circle Your Answer.

Going Slow				Steady				Aggressive

Re-Examining Your Deadline

Do you have a deadline? _____

Are you on track with your deadline? _____

Do you need to speed up to catch up? _____

Do you need to re-adjust your deadline? _____

Remember: Your approach will determine your deadline!

3 Writing Relationship Points

1. **You Must Show Up!** ~ **Circle Your Answer.**

Have you been showing up consistently to write?   Yes   or   No.

When and what time is your NEXT writing date?

_____

2. Keep Choosing Each Other!

What sacrifice did you make in order to write today?

_____

_____

3. Keep Your Eyes Focused ~ Distractions Must Go!

Write a list of the things that do distract you or have distracted you?

_____	_____
_____	_____
_____	_____
_____	_____

Remember: Distractions Must Go!

What is your plan to deal with these distractions?

_____

_____

_____

_____

_____

You Must Keep Your Eyes Focused and Stay Determined.

Remember: Your completed manuscript is your finish line.

YOU CAN DO IT!

Assignment: Read pages 25 through 27 in 'Somebody Please Help Me To Write Book' 1st before answering the questions.

Your Writing Communication Examination

Has your writing been flowing? _____   Are you still writing? _____

<u>If you answered yes, continue on to the next section on page 23.</u>

If you no to any of these questions, then it is time to stop and examine where you are.

#1 Tip On How To Re-examine Your Writing Communication

EXAMINE YOUR OUTLINE AND DETERMINE WHERE YOU ARE

What on your outline have you already completed?

_____

_____

_____

_____

Where do you need to start writing?

_____

_____

_____

A Tip To Keep Your Writing Relationship Fresh

- **Explore new things that bring a fresh perspective to the relationship.**

    - Vision Boarding

    - Timed Writing

    - Listen to Related Topic Conversations

- Which of these approaches will you try and why?

_____

_____

_____

_____

What was the result?

_____

_____

_____

_____

NOW BACK TO WRITING!

If you need help, reach out to us at <u>kingdomwriters2017@gmail.com</u>, or Kingdom Writers Books on Facebook

Encouraging The 'Writer' In You

Assignment: Read pages 29 through 32 in 'Somebody Please Help Me To Write Book' 1st before answering the questions.

- ### It's The Bravest Thing I've Ever Done

Writing Your Book is one of the Bravest Things You have ever done.

Name a few other things you have done.

_____

_____

_____

Add 'Writing My Book' to the bottom of the list.

- ### I Can Make A Difference (Yes You Can!)

You began writing because you have a message or story that you want to use to make a difference in someone else's life.

Think about a time when you made a difference in someone else's life.

*Write briefly about it. *

_____

_____

_____

- **I Can Make It Happen**

You can do this by making your writing happen each and every day.

*Name a relationship that you consider important in your life. *

_____

_____

How important is this relationship to you?

_____

_____

What do you do to exemplify how important this relationship is in your life?

_____

_____

What can you do differently to treat your writing the same way?

_____

_____

Treat Your Writing The Same Way. ~You Can Make It Happen

- **I'm Just One Person, But An Important Person**

Name some important people in your life.

_____

_____

_____

_____

Why are the people you listed important?

_____

_____

_____

_____

Now add your name at the end of the list.

How does your name being on the list make you feel?

~Write It Here!

_____

_____

_____

Remember: You are just as important as everyone else on your list.

- **Every day Is A Great Day To Write**

1. Pull out your calendar. If you don't have one write down your schedule for the week here!

   Monday:_____

   Tuesday:_____

   Wednesday:_____

   Thursday:_____

   Friday:_____

   Saturday:_____

   Sunday:_____

2. Look for additional opportunities hidden within your schedule to write. Write Them Here!

   _____   _____

   _____   _____

   _____   _____

   _____   _____

3. When is or was your scheduled time to write today?

   _____

4. What is or was the weather today?

   _____

5. Did you find additional time(s) in your schedule today to write?

   _____

6. Did you keep your scheduled writing time today?

   _____

7. Did you keep your additional times of writing for today?

   _____

8. Do you have your scheduled times and additional times for the rest of the week? _____

9. Repeat these steps each week to help keep track of your writing journey.

10. Say this affirmation today: **'Everyday Is A Great Day To Write.'**

    Then repeat this affirmation every day.

I Must Show Up

When is the deadline for your book?

_____

Can you image others reading your story?

_____

_____

Who is your audience (niche)?

_____

_____

Refresh: Write your reason for writing your book.

_____

_____

_____

Keep that image and vision in front of you everyday.

- **Additional Affirmations**

Now it's time for you to write your own affirmations that help encourage yourself through your writing journey.

_____

_____

NOW BACK TO WRITING!

Help My Writing, Pleasee!

Assignment: Read pages 33 through 35 in 'Somebody Please Help Me To Write Book' 1st before answering the questions.

- **Understand, It Is Work.**

Do you work a full-time job? _____

Circle the words that describe how you feel about your job?

RELAXING   **FUN**   **ENCOURAGING**   **HEALING**

TEDIOUS   **LABOR-SOME**   **DRAINING**   **FULFILLING**

EXCITING

Since you have started writing, circle the words that describe how you feel about your writing process.

RELAXING   **FUN**   **ENCOURAGING**   **HEALING**

TEDIOUS   **LABOR-SOME**   **DRAINING**   **FULFILLING**

EXCITING

Do you see any similarities? _____

Do you see any major differences? _____

List any positive feedback you have received while on your writing journey.

_____
_____
_____
_____

Stay on course, keep accomplishing the task and you will reach your end result.

- **How Do I Communicate?**

How well are you communicating your message to your audience?

~ Answer the following questions.

1. Are you keeping your audience in mind as you write or have you just been focusing on writing?

_____
_____

2. What is the message of your book?

_____
_____

3. Is your message clear throughout your book?

_____

4. Write out the major points of the message in your book here.

_____

_____

_____

_____

5. What was your writing process approach? ~ **Circle Your Answers.**

          DIRECT   OR   SUBTLE

6. Does your ending drive home your message?   YES   OR   NO

7. Who is your audience?

_____

_____

8. Based on your answers to the above questions, are you on track?

          YES   OR   NO

If not, you need to revamp your writing process. What changes will you make?

_____

_____

_____

_____

• Your Attitude, Your Approach, Your Writing

Attitude Check ~ **Answer the following questions.**

1. What is your attitude towards your writing right now?

   _____

   _____

   _____

2. What words do you literally speak about your writing process?

   _____

   _____

   _____

3. Do you notice a trend? ~ **Circle Your Answer**

   POSITIVE   OR   NEGATIVE

4. Describe the attitude you have when you sit down to write.

   _____

   _____

   _____

If you notice a negative attitude, then it is time to change it.

Write down any new observations you notice about your attitude changes towards your writing journey.

_____

_____

_____

_____

_____

_____

Journal here any other thoughts you have during your writing journey.

_____

_____

_____

_____

_____

_____

Don't let the circumstances around you affect your writing attitude.

Assignment: Read pages 35 through 41 in 'Somebody Please Help Me To Write Book' 1st before answering the questions.

Pay Attention

Pay Attention To The Direction Of Your Writing

Is your writing relevant to the section you are writing in?

_____

Does your writing have nothing to do with the section that you are currently writing in?

_____

_____

Take a moment to review your writing to see if you need if you need to make a change in direction.

⬆

Were you going up or down? _____

⬇

Do you need to change directions? _____

THIS IS YOUR FRIENDLY REMINDER!

BE YOU

AUTHOR ~ READER ~CONNECTION

BE YOURSELF WHEN WRITING YOUR MESSAGE OR STORY

Examine Your Writing.

Does your writing really connect with your readers?

_____

_____

_____

_____

Are you relatable? _____

Are you personable? _____

ONLY BE YOU. DON'T TRY TO WRITE LIKE ANYONE ELSE.

EXPRESS YOURSELF

YOUR VOICE   PLUS   YOUR HEART   EQUALS   EXPRESSION

Let someone you trust read a chapter or section of your book.

Can they hear your heart and passion in your book?

Circle: YES   OR   NO

Does Your Message Come Through In Your Book?

Circle: YES   OR   NO

If they answered YES, skip to the next section on page 40.

If they answered NO to those two questions, read and complete the following 7 steps:

1. Stop and re-read what you have already wrote

2. Listen for the person of your writing. Does it should like you speaking?

3. Is your message coming through?

4. Do you hear your own heart and passion in what you have already written?

5. If not, think about re-writing those parts in your own voice. Write it how you would say it.

6. Re-read what you just wrote, do you notice a difference?

7. Now continue writing.

HAPPY WRITING!

Help Me I'm Stuck!

Refer back to your OUTLINE

Take a moment to consult your guide.

Write your outline here using this blank space:

Circle what you have finished. What's left is where you need to start.

If you need additional space, use separate sheets of paper.

Now, where do you need to add section titles or subheadings?

Write them here.

_____

_____

_____

_____

_____

If you are complete. Next read through everything you wrote start to finish. Take brief notes of what you need to add or delete here.

_____

_____

_____

_____

_____

_____

_____

If there is no spark, reach to us at kingdomwriters2017@gmail.com

Oh No! I Missed My Writing Date!

It's not too late to write. Follow these 8 steps to make up for it.

1. Pull out your schedule or write down your schedule for that day only.

2. Seek out 20-30 minutes or more of free time.

3. Write in that slot, 'WRITING DATE.' Fill up all the slots you can in your schedule for that day with that.

4. Now, keep that schedule where you can see it.

5. Set your alarm on your phone for those times.

6. When the alarm goes out at those times, stop, pull out your notebook, pen/pencil and WRITE.

7. REPEAT steps 5-7 for all the other times you set for that day.

8. Afterwards, check your schedule for tomorrow's writing date and set your alarms.

REMEMBER: 'Some Writing Is Better Than No Writing.'

~ Erica Rutherford

Need help, reach out to us at <u>kingdomwriters2017@gmail.com</u>

Did My Help Forsake Me?

Answer the following questions. ~ Write Your Answers.

Are you using a Ghostwriter or another helper?

_____

****IF NOT, THEN SKIP AHEAD TO THE NEXT SECTION ON PAGE 45.****
IF SO, CONTINUE TO THE NEXT QUESTION.

Do you hear from them regularly or does it seems like they have forgotten about you?

_____

Does your ghostwriter or helper take your book serious?

_____

What's the progress of your book from the time you last worked with them?

_____

_____

DON'T LET THEM FORGET ABOUT YOU.

Here are 6 steps to use evaluate your connection and book status with them.

1. Pick up the phone and call them

2. Send an email and wait for a reply

3. Pay them a visit if this was established in the beginning of the relationship.

4. Have them give you an update about the status of your book.

5. Remind them of the agreement or contract (if applicable)

6. If they are not fulfilling their part of the agreement, fire them if you must.

7. Seek out another credentialed ghostwriter or helper you trust.

Did You Complete Any Of These Steps? _____

If So, Which Ones? _____

Is Your Writing Back On Track Now? _____

Stay Connected With Them Through Your Book Writing Process.

Get Your Writing Done!

When The Bitter End Is The Sweetest

You are almost to the finish line.

How do you feel right now?

_____

_____

_____

What are you working on finishing up?

_____

_____

_____

Are you struggling? ~Circle One.   YES   OR   NO

The Answer?????

Change Your View!!!!

Read and Recite the Following 'I CAN' Statements

I CAN bring a closure to my story or message.

I CAN complete what I started

I CAN complete my book.

I CAN complete my book.

How do you feel after reading these statements? ~Write It.

_____

What is your plan to finish writing? ~Write It!

_____

_____

_____

_____

Now execute your plan to finish strong. You're Almost Done. Go! Go!

It's A Wrap! ~ You Finished!

Assignment: Read page 43 in 'Somebody Please Help Me To Write Book' 1st before answering the questions.

Congratulations

YOU DID IT!!!!!

What parts did you enjoy?

_____

_____

_____

Did you find anything bitter about your process?

_____

_____

_____

Was the process worth it?

_____

_____

_____

NOW IT'S TIME TO CELEBRATE!

- Be proud of yourself and your accomplishment

- Celebrate

- Pat yourself on your back

- Catch up on any naps or sleep you may have missed out on

- Do some other things for a min. You earned it!

- Finally, prepare to move forward to get your book published

I Personally Congratulate You. I Personally Celebrate You.

You Did It. You Accomplished It.

You Are Officially An Author Now.

About The Authors

Erica Rutherford is an author, minister, musician, songwriter, praise dancer, praise and worship leader, speaker, teacher residing in Central Indiana with her husband, Lewis C Rutherford Jr. Erica is a motivated driven leader that has been called to encourage and empower the people of God in this hour through her music, teachings, dance and writings. Erica and her husband are currently working on their 1st CD, 2 song collaborations and their next book 'No More Egypt.'

Erica has traveled some of the world as a classical violinist. Erica now does freelance music in the genres of gospel, inspirational and jazz. In her free time, Erica enjoys crafting, knitting, video and board games, hanging with friends, learning new things and traveling.

Erica can be reached her Facebook account name: EricaGodschildRutherford, or the Kingdom Writers Books page, at the Kingdom Writers Books website: www.bit.ly/kingdomwritersbooks and at the Kingdom Writers Books email: kingdomwriters2017@gmail.com. You can visit Amazon.com, Barnes&Noble.com or contact her personally to purchase her books.

Lewis C Rutherford Jr. is an minister, singer, songwriter, musician and author residing in central Indiana with his wife Erica A Rutherford. Lewis is a high energy passionate leader that is called to encourage and empower the people of God in this hour through his music, teachings and his writings. Lewis and his wife are currently working on their 1st CD, 2 song collaborations and their next book 'No More Egypt.'

Lewis has traveled the world participating in various music conferences and events. Lewis does freelance music mainly in the genres of inspirational, gospel and jazz. In his free time, Lewis enjoys video and board games, learning and trying new things, hanging with friends, and traveling.

Lewis can be reach at his Gmail account name: Gospodj@gmail.com or at the Kingdom Writers Book's email: kingdomwriters2017@gmail.com , and at the Kingdom Writer's Books website: www.bit.ly/kingdomwritersbooks you can visit Amazon.com, Barnes&Noble.com or contact him personally to purchase his books.

Bonuses:

Private Facebook Group On-going Access. Email us for access.

Purchase through: Amazon, Barnes and Nobles,

our website: www.bit.ly/kingdomwritersbooks

Also Available on eBook

Contact us for your signed copy today.

Get a Free copy of our ebooks: '6 Daily Steps to Help You Start Writing' and 'A Writer's Guide For Writing' when purchasing a signed copy from us.

www.ingramcontent.com/pod-product-compliance
Lightning Source LLC
Chambersburg PA
CBHW082255220526
45469CB00009B/3016